Lowriders

By Danny Parr

Reading Consultant:
Dr. Robert Miller
Professor of Special Education
Minnesota State University, Mankato

CAPSTONE
HIGH-INTEREST
BOOKS

an imprint of Capstone Press
Mankato, Minnesota

Capstone High-Interest Books are published by Capstone Press
151 Good Counsel Drive, P.O. Box 669, Mankato, Minnesota 56002
http://www.capstone-press.com

Library of Congress Cataloging-in-Publication Data
Parr, Danny.
    Lowriders/by Danny Parr.
    p. cm.—(Wild rides)
    Includes bibliographical references and index.
    ISBN 0-7368-0928-7
    1. Lowriders—Juvenile literature. 2. Mexican Americans—Juvenile
literature. [1. Lowriders. 2. Automobiles—Customizing.] I. Title. II. Series.
TL255.2 .P37 2002
629.28'72—dc21   2001000211

Summary: Discusses these customized vehicles, their history, parts, and the
artwork with which owners decorate them.

Editorial Credits
Matt Doeden, editor; Karen Risch, product planning editor; Kia Bielke,
    cover and interior designer; Katy Kudela, photo researcher

Photo Credits
Harris from Paris, 8, 22 (top), 25
Isaac Hernandez/Mercury Press, 14–15, 16 (top), 16 (bottom), 21, 26, 28
Peter S. Ford, cover, 13
Unicorn Stock Photos/Dennis Thompson, 18
www.ronkimball/stock.com, 4 (top), 4 (bottom), 7, 10, 22 (bottom)

1 2 3 4 5 6 07 06 05 04 03 02

Table of Contents

Learn about:

Customization

Paint jobs

Dancing
competitions

CHAPTER **1**

Lowriders

Three judges gather around a lowrider named Pure Insanity. This vehicle once was a standard 1983 Chevrolet S-10 pickup. But the truck's owners changed its appearance. It now looks very different from other S-10 trucks. It is now a lowrider.

The judges carry lists of items to check on Pure Insanity. They notice all of the changes the truck's owners have made. The judges check the style of the doors and windows. They look closely at the truck's paint job. They notice how low the truck sits to the ground. The judges make notes as they look over Pure Insanity. They like what they see. The judges decide to give Pure Insanity's owners an award for their hard work.

About Lowriders

Lowriders are vehicles that have been customized by their owners. An owner who customizes a vehicle makes changes in the vehicle's appearance. Owners create vehicles to suit their personality. All lowriders sit low to the ground. The name "lowrider" comes from this feature.

Owners customize their lowriders with special paint jobs. Some owners use one solid color. Others use many colors. Owners may paint words or pictures on the hood or sides of a lowrider. These features help owners create different and interesting vehicles.

Almost any vehicle can become a lowrider. Cars and trucks are the most common lowriders. But people also can make lowriders out of vehicles such as vans and motorcycles.

Lowrider Competitions

Lowrider owners take part in a variety of competitions. Many of these competitions take place at car shows.

Judges look at all of the lowriders in a show. They give awards to the best vehicles in different classes. For example, judges may give an award to the best truck. They may give another award to the lowrider with the best paint job.

Lowriders sit low to the ground.

In hop competitions, drivers use hydraulics to make lowriders' front tires lift off the ground.

Hydraulic Competitions

Lowrider owners also may take part in competitions that show off their hydraulic systems. These devices allow lowrider drivers to raise and lower their vehicles' front and back ends. Hydraulic competitions include hopping and dancing.

In hop competitions, drivers use hydraulics to make lowriders' front tires briefly lift off the ground. The drivers try to make their lowriders' tires hop as high as they can. The lowrider that hops the highest wins the competition.

Drivers in dancing competitions use hydraulic systems to make their lowriders rise and fall to music. The lowriders appear to be dancing. Judges give each driver a score based on the lowrider's moves.

Learn about:

Barrios

Lead sleds

First modern lowrider

CHAPTER 2

Early Models of Lowriders

Many people in the United States bought new cars in the late 1940s. During World War II (1939–1945), the U.S. military needed many of the materials used for building new cars. Many people did not buy new cars during the war. They waited until the war was over.

Some people could not afford new cars. Others wanted cars that no one else had. Some of these people bought old cars and modified them. They changed the cars to match their personalities. They then gathered to show off their cars to one another.

The First Lowriders

In the 1950s, the first lowriders were built in the Mexican American neighborhoods of southern California. These neighborhoods sometimes were called "barrios." This word means "neighborhood" in Spanish.

Many people from the barrios bought old cars. The cars were large and heavy. Some people called these cars "lead sleds." Lead sleds were strong and heavy like lead metal.

Owners changed the cars to make them lower to the ground. They sometimes put sandbags in the trunks. The sandbags made the cars' back ends sink lower to the ground. People began calling the drivers of these cars "lowriders."

Some owners lowered the back ends too much. The bottoms of the cars sometimes would scrape the road. Many state and local governments then passed laws that prevented owners from lowering their cars too far.

Lowrider owners often drove around their towns to show off their cars.

Modern Lowriders

A Los Angeles man named Raul Agguirre had an idea about customizing his car. He wanted a car that sat high when he drove around the streets of Los Angeles. But he wanted it to sit low when parked.

Agguirre knew about hydraulic systems on airplanes and delivery trucks. He had seen how these systems easily moved heavy objects up and down. Agguirre added a hydraulic system

to his 1954 Chevrolet Corvette. It became the first modern lowrider.

Lowrider owners continued to search for ways to change their cars. Some owners tried customizing new models of cars. They changed cars made by manufacturers such as Honda and Mazda. Other owners gave old cars new looks. For example, some owners added tiny tires to large cars.

Most modern lowriders have hydraulic systems to move the cars up and down.

Learn about:

Dropping the vehicle

Hydraulic systems

Paint jobs

CHAPTER **3**

CALIFORNIA
4T96881

Designing a Lowrider

Lowrider owners begin with standard vehicles. Almost any vehicle can become a lowrider. But cars and trucks are the most common lowriders. Two popular models for lowriders are the 1936 Ford and the 1952 Mercury.

Owners first drop a vehicle to make it a lowrider. They modify the suspension system to drop a vehicle. This system connects the main body of the car to the wheels. The body also is called the chassis. The chassis rests on springs. These springs control how high above the ground the chassis sits. Designers may replace existing springs with short springs so the vehicle is closer to the ground. This is called dropping the vehicle.

Hydraulic Systems and Air Bags

Most lowriders have hydraulic systems. Owners add cylinders to each wheel. These tube-shaped containers hold hydraulic fluid. The cylinders are connected to powerful batteries. Pumps push the hydraulic fluid inside the cylinders.

Layers of paint and lacquer make lowriders look shiny.

The force of the fluid causes the vehicle to go up and down.

Some lowriders have air bags instead of hydraulic systems. Owners add an air bag to each wheel. They put an air tank and an air compressor under the car. The tank connects to each of the air bags. Drivers flip a switch to pump air into the bags to move the vehicle up. Another switch allows them to release air from the bags to move the vehicle down.

Appearance

Appearance is the most important lowrider feature. Owners work hard to make their lowriders look good. They try to build unique vehicles. They want their designs to stand out from those of other lowrider owners.

Many of the changes designers make to lowriders affect only appearance. Owners pay special attention to paint jobs. They may choose bright colors for the lowrider's body. Owners often apply many coats of paint to a lowrider. They then add layers of clear lacquer. This coating makes the paint look shiny.

Exterior Changes

Owners also customize a vehicle's exterior features. They may add "suicide" doors. These doors open from the front of the vehicle instead of the back. Suicide doors are dangerous for road vehicles. They can easily hurt a driver during a crash. But some lowrider owners like the way the doors look.

Designers may customize many other features of a lowrider. They may add fancy door handles or old-fashioned fenders. Some designers add expensive hood ornaments.

Interior Changes

Owners also pay close attention to the inside of lowriders. They decorate the seats, walls, and floor with soft, colorful fabric. Velvet and velour fabrics are common in lowrider interiors.

Owners may add other interior features. They may add gold-plated fixtures or shiny chrome knobs. They may cover the steering wheel in soft fabric. Some designers even include TV sets or fish aquariums in the back seat.

The sound system is an important lowrider feature. Early lowrider owners sometimes drove their vehicles around while playing loud music on the radio. Lowrider owners may add expensive CD players and speakers to their vehicles. Some lowriders include 20 or more speakers.

Owners also work to make the lowrider's engine look good. They keep the engine very clean. They may add chromc to engine parts. During car shows, they sometimes place mirrors under the vehicle to show off the entire engine.

Owners may decorate the interiors of their lowriders with soft, colorful fabric.

Learn about:

Regional differences

Ways to customize

Types of lowriders

CHAPTER **4**

Customizing Lowriders

Lowrider owners want interesting and unique designs for their vehicles. Many owners do all of their own customizing. They enjoy doing the work themselves. Owners sometimes let friends and family members help them customize their lowriders.

New Mexico Lowriders

People in certain areas sometimes customize their lowriders in a similar way. New Mexico is one such region. Many lowriders there have a similar look.

New Mexico lowriders often are old vehicles. Owners frequently paint religious images on their vehicles. They may paint Biblical figures such as Jesus Christ or the Virgin Mary. Owners may use chain-link steering wheels that represent the rosary. Many people of the Catholic religion use these strings of beads in prayer.

Chonca Montoya owns a New Mexico lowrider. Montoya believes that her lowrider is a way to express her religion. Montoya's 1977 Thunderbird includes a painting of her church on the hood. The trunk features a painting of Jesus knocking on a door.

Southern California Lowriders

Many lowrider owners in southern California build lowriders from smaller, newer cars and trucks. They often use vehicles built in Europe or Japan. These vehicles have a smooth, narrow appearance. Many owners in southern California paint shocking designs on their lowriders. Southern California lowriders may feature paintings of figures such as pirates or the devil.

Donny Bowers owns a 1995 Honda Accord lowrider named V-tec Vengeance. The front and rear bumpers are molded to the fenders.

This shape gives the car a smooth look. Many small skulls are painted on the inside and the outside of the car. One large skull is painted on the hood.

Southern California lowriders often feature shocking designs.

Owners think of their lowriders as works of art.

Other Designs

Lowrider owners do not have to follow any set style. They can customize their lowriders in whatever way they like. People have many ways of making their lowriders unique.

Some owners use their lowriders to honor people. They may paint images of friends or family members. Some paint images of famous people such as Elvis on their lowriders. Others honor groups of people such as war veterans.

Lowriders are more than just vehicles to their owners. People spend thousands of dollars customizing their lowriders. Owners think of each vehicle as a work of art.

Gypsy Rose

Gypsy Rose is one of the world's most famous lowriders. Jesse Valadez built Gypsy Rose from a 1964 Chevrolet Impala. He painted 150 roses on the car. He used dark pink velvet fabric for the interior. He even replaced the interior lights with small hanging lamps called chandeliers.

Gypsy Rose quickly became one of the most popular lowriders in North America. In the mid-1970s, the producers of the TV show *Chico and the Man* saw the car. They asked Valadez if they could include it at the beginning of each show. Soon, Gypsy Rose was the most recognized lowrider in North America.

Words to Know

chassis (CHASS-ee)—the frame on which the body of a vehicle is built

chrome (KROHM)—a coating of a metallic substance called chromium; chrome gives objects a shiny, metallic appearance.

customize (KUHSS-tuh-mize)—to change a vehicle's appearance

hydraulic system (hye-DRAW-lik SISS-tuhm)—an automotive system powered by fluid forced through chambers or pipes

lacquer (LAK-ur)—a clear liquid coating applied to lowriders to give them a shiny appearance

modify (MOD-uh-fye)—to change; people modify a car or engine in order to make it faster or more powerful.

suspension system (suh-SPEN-shuhn SISS-tuhm)—the system of springs and shock absorbers that absorbs up-and-down movement from the axles

velour (vuh-LOOR)—a soft, thick fabric designed to resemble velvet

To Learn More

Lake, E. D. *Lowriders.* Wheels. Mankato, Minn.: Capstone Books, 1995.

Parr, Danny. *Lowriders.* Race Car Legends. Philadelphia: Chelsea House, 2000.

Werther, Scott P. *Low Riders.* Extreme Machines. New York: PowerKids Press, 2001.

Useful Addresses

Lowrider Magazine
Lowrider Publishing Group
2100 East Howell Avenue
Anaheim, CA 92806

Street Customs Magazine
P.O. Box 3446
Whittier, CA 90605

Internet Sites

BumpStop.com
http://www.bumpstop.com/menu.htm

Lowrider Magazine
http://www.lowridermagazine.com/main.shtml

Index